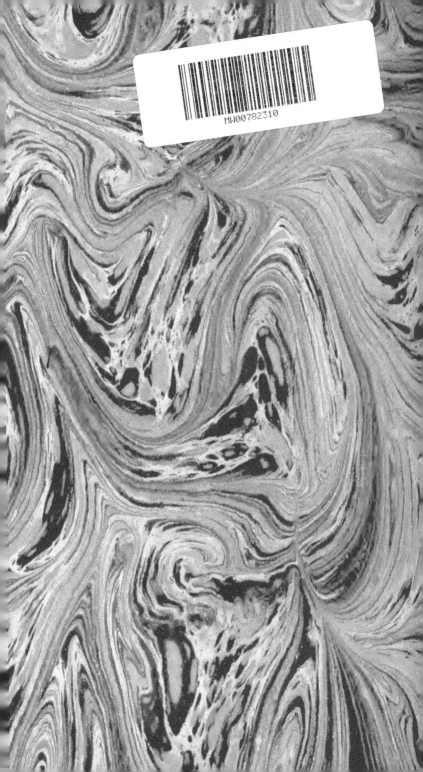
MW00782310

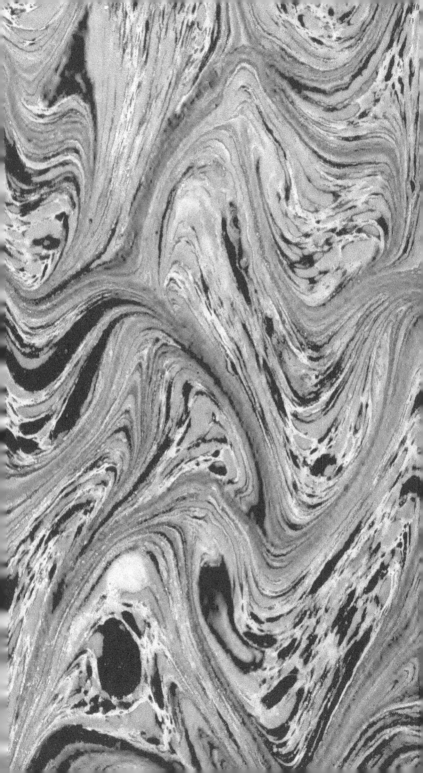

cauldrons

K.R. MORRISON

cauldrons

K.R. MORRISON

Paper Press

cauldrons
K.R. Morrison © 2021

Thank you to
Haight Ashbury Literary Journal, Quiet Lightning, Gasconade Review, and
Bay Area Generations
where some of these poems first appeared.

Use of cover image diamondring.jpg
provided by general GNU license, Wikimedia.org

Initial edits by Paul Corman-Roberts
Editing, artwork, and print design by Youssef Alaoui
Paper Press Books & Assoc. Publishing Co.
978-0-615-86874-5

A   P   A   P   E   R
P   R   E   S   S   B   O   O   K

To uncle "Big J,"
for stirring me to write
for your love & friction

cauldrons

Foreword

Sweep the space with water and sea salt.
Light the candle.
Create a wisdom circle and let the poems enter.

KR Morrison is writing the life ceremonial and
improvisational. She explores the corners created
by moon cultures meeting sun cultures: the blue
moon, the black moon, the cauldron's belly.

The child watches as the cauldron is stirred, wants
to touch the wisdom as it heats, and is burned by it,
changed by it.

Cauldron of ocean where it meets shore, and
Morrison reminds us, "in sea foam reside night
witch ghosts."

I wonder, dear reader, if you have breathed through
a conjuration. I wonder if you have conjured
yourself.

"Fear not those old soul tangles" KR croons in a
resonant voice, the voice of the Bone Mother.
Later the pirate self untangles knots.

The night that I wrote this, in the dark moon, a
frog sang into the fogdark. I don't ever remember
hearing a frog on this hillside before. Sometimes
the moon is a frog mother. These poems remind us
to listen, to be present.

Morrison is teacher, poet, and witch. She is moon and mix and writes from the crossroads of origin and heart. She is mother restless, soldier souled and a child apart.

"We swap lost verbs, we slip consonance" her drummer's spirit calls us. Who knows what sisters will answer this time.

K Shuck
7th Poet Laureate of San Francisco
April, in the second year of the pandemic

Contents

A ſcepter.

A ſword.

A ſcourge.

Charlotte Ann

like mother—like daughter
I never know
what waterbeds or polluted men
need a lesson
from a drifting bullet

today I tell your stories

who knows what's true
from the fiction your scars harbor
for a fallen woman's final justice

today I walk barefoot for you
I harbor homemade tortillas
in my heart I never
did taste, I bleed out
this world loaded with a .38

the poet in me thinks that just like you
make-believe and memory
can make a homemade meal in 20 minutes

to feed double shift mothers
to nourish street sons, bruised daughters
your ever evicted stove
of legacies dancing
in lard laden frying pans

today I walk barefoot
and the souls of my feet bleed
so I walk stronger, I smile
remembering a little girl you enlisted
to rub your pirate black feet

I walk barefoot on the bones of your words—

you're good, Babygirl. But your sister,
she has those softball hands.
She can rub some feet.

so I worked harder
on your soles harboring whiskied men, fists
and marbled in the madness, so much
broken glass mixed with moonstone
so much soul and sadness

Funny what a mother can do.
She can return to smiles
set the tone, salvage
love inside knee scabs
while she loses raising you

Her Altar

Your pictures come first
     cascades of you
          that testify, language

Can't touch what a pirate woman
     weathers and braves
          her Grand Canyon narrative

Hiked so ordinary souls
     can stretch, bleed
          a little, digest

Then come your favorite things
     Supremes records
          your Lakers t-shirt

Chevrolet, steak and eggs
     Folgers Coffee and Wild Turkey
          your sacred Trail of Tears

Around moonrise, candles converge
     a bone echo of your voice returns, lost
          daughters come, thirsty for a nest

A broken man, he lost his mother
     I watch his tears
          rest in your sunset hands

The smell of motorcycle engines
     polished oak and gun metal
          wrap around him like a moon blanket

A little girl
  climbs inside portraits of you
    Is this your mom? she asks

  Her questions kiss
    your paintings and photographs
      my grandma went to heaven too

  she adds. She declares her muerta dress
    I stitched it myself, on my mom's sewing
      machine she says, her green

      eyes
        fastened
          to you

I retreat to all those costumes
  you handmade for us kids –
    my brother a clown

My sister a Cherokee warrior
  on Hallow's Eve – I visit
    those sandboxed visits

A sad child's playground
  rusty swings chained to first love lost
    I hated the world

      didn't get along
        with you

A policeman
        clears his throat
                a cold disruption

                        Ma'am, it's time to break down.
                        Pack it up. Time for you to go
                        home.

Home. My eyes find callous
        hands, wrapped around a flashlight
                and a gun strap, bury

Home on wounded knee
        your countless evictions
                a rental—an emotion—a relationship

I blow out the candles, I say goodbye
        Like leaving you on weekends, an ache
                looms in my lungs, outweighs me

I collect you, pictures and offerings
        as if I'm packing a life
                time of our conversations

I feel our Mother Moon hold me
        as if I'm a foster child
                my new address, All Soul's Day

Her Burden

In one week, a woman
     can grow life
          shoot a rapist   bleed out

     the last word
          while he leaks red hell

          on car fenders   she waxes
          when she isn't waning

In one week, a woman
     can talk tears off suicidal bridges
          while she bridges

          words to new days
          dressed in smiles   preparing

          breakfast mixed with messages
          self discovery over easy
          pancakes that make pain too, pass

In one week, a woman can become
     an armed robber   or she can

     nurse bottles and beers
     (and in the same week)
     bring freedom to kids   she never raised
                            but carries

While vacuuming others' mess, a woman
        can write a poem

        on hallways she architects
        inside her head

        that always   she revises
                           surveillances

She can burn
        down the world
                with flammable honesty

                then discover fire
                extinguishers

                while men
                cough, choke, drop
                for cover

Bone Mother

at a crossroads, She meets you in shadows
      Dark Moon Mother
together you walk through dead battles
      old scars scattered in nightlands
cold like bones at your feet, like bones

      holding stories, eras old
you're ready to shed, bones
      holding magick, new phases
await so next to Her, you shed
      your baby moon skin

in Her shadowlands, you hear ancestors
      hymning, behind them Bone Mother
the Night Queen of the Crossroads sings

fear not those old soul tangles, leave
the past at Mother Earth's feet
I have you witch daughter, shed
that little girl free, let your Divine
bloom, give all that death to me

8 Hour Shift

Mother Moon
She is a Mistress

She spreads her legs
around Gustav Klimt prints
nailed to burgundy bedrooms

She wraps her ivory velvet thighs
around one woman awake
beneath stained sheets, cold love
replaced by remnant nightfall, wet violet

Mother Moon charges by the hour
even for a harmless dance. For full price
she sends mariachis to balconies unswept
conjuring hearts starving
lovers blue balled and bereft

For a little less she hovers
broken hearted tongues suck salt left
between her breasts, her Moon blood
womb swooning for love inside sex
lonely and cauldroned, conjuring

Mother Moon naked blue
arouses red inside my flesh, left

sticky by Her librations
I hear my backbone think

My nightlight Mother
I smell you on my flesh
when I awake to the daytime dead

Mother Moon, always a pleasure
our business in my bed

Sea Babies

she feeds him dark honey
from her mouth

lip couplets watch words
withdraw, wait their turn

Moon & Sun write notes
to her thighs, to his hands

under his bear lungs, she finds
buried a large nautilus, inside

its spirals, she hears
owls singing, signaling her

to swallow him, his brown
skin, salvage his heart

parts sunk below
his upset, seabed stomach

inhale his silent mind, hold
thoughts as he holds his breath

he feeds her homemade soup
from an amethyst nest

abrasions drown, her
fixed scars unhook, sink

Moon & Sun summon
two sea babies within

hands stirring, thighs sirening

Silver Lining

Silver lines are the black sandpaper circles
    on my feet soles, distanced I walk
        and work and bleed barefoot, grounding

Silver lines are found dangling
    in Venice's emerald and jade canals
        village kids catch sterling, touristless

        some kind of new currency
        stuffed in green's soul pockets

Silver is the aged son
    forced back into dad's house, cooking roots
        recipes, raking leaves

        seven generations of ancestor lineage
        healing accidentally

Silver is the line of daughters ready to redefine
    breeding, armies
        masked Lady Vikings
        preparing

        the Scumgirl overthrow

Silver lining is us, skylines of poets
    meeting in cyber luna cloud attics

in moon space

we swap lost verbs, we slip consonance
into lonely's argent tongue

Silver lining are musicians
    quarantined, hibernating
        in vinyl strewn bedrooms, strumming

        up buried lockets, inside rust hides
        new transitions, songs awakening

Silver linings are the circus mirrors
    in which we find our bruised selves
        from ego we jailbreak

        like raw, thirsty
        geodes facing
        tired illusions, we dust off

        soot from our shadows, urge
        our inner child to color outside
        her silver maiden lines

        paint nameless shades
        into next level
        crone chapters

in sea foam reside past lives

horses tire of racing just to lose
so they dive from the iron box

sirens from Istanbul
their souls charcoal and pruned

tribes of children awaiting return, youth
spirit guides for men who fail

to pick Love, bleeding dead
flies from patriarchy's tongue

in sea foam reside night witch ghosts

sour waves reek of ancestor mistakes
in moon wind I smell hexes

curses stuck in my throat
a bitter coven's whiskey breath

in sea foam reside warriors

who pledged
the wrong allegiance

purple hearts tangled
to rusty anchors, they drown

in their honorable discharges, old lies
uniformed in hero epithets

in sea foam I see me

四 four maybe five, wild red
curls over blue, moon bone skin

baby me, listen close to their death hymns
build their regrets into sea castles

baby me, carve
their restless wishes

                    spirals
                        in the sand

Witch Poet

Before he hijacked her diction
she wrote for topics that matter —

      Mother's starving
      for more wombs
      black eyed bruisers
      and scathed street kids
      wishes blocked from sunburns
      worded by winter

Now, under his spell
her word revolutions wait
while she prostitutes
for male pronouns.

But poets needn't worry —

      Whores either die or they recover
      in the wake of a heretic's regret
      they resurrect as a Serengeti elephant

      Guiding damaged girls back to dictionaries
      for a little witchcraft, for a cauldron
      stinking of rich diction, self-respect

      Strong blood from her pen returns her
      to summon Amazons, haunting him

in sleep, in manuscripts

Her words. Such spells
escort her back, her words
burn him in the fire
she conjured him —

Sacrament

if he's not careful

      all these hurting
      girls with moon cycles

will collect her monthly
red juju into mason jars
like magick ruby bullets

      she will
      phase him away

with buried poppets, armed
and charmed he will end
by her Holy Blood

One Nation, Under Murder

i hear ancestors
    beneath my skin, southern dead

sing heavenly hymns, i clench grief
    & boil, blisters rise from my deerskin fists

lovers can't breathe, i hold my breath
    whips possess my nails, slice lynched

ghosts into my flesh, i smell spells here, inhale
    the conjuring, breathe out the casting

revolution & reform argue at a dinner table
    like a tired couple, their marriage arranged

> *Daughter Justice rolls her eyes, dresses*
> *in a wardrobe that's restless, she itches*
> *to break curfew, curses "progress"*
> *she envisions beyond their food at the table*

i hear karmic returns hatching
    so many seeds sprouting, loud

flowers blooming from systemic stems
    from brave weeds, i hear scar anthems sprouting

some of us march, our bone collections stir
    orbit storms, we take bullets for too many dead

some of us harbor graveyards in our stomachs
    for Justice, we bury our silence

under America's democracy dirt
        for Justice, we turn blue

        we hold our breath

Rune

I cast nine switchblades

>   made of my skin, black cactus
>   reminders I bury in you

I resurrect in memory basements

>   my naked ghost dances
>   ice cold footprints

>   through your backbone
>   mazes. I kick rocks

>   turn over stones, I graffiti soul
>   ruins so those Conquistadoras

>   smell our magick
>   so your wounds know

I cast nine gritas

>   in you, bruja echoes
>   for every poema that holds you

>   like my bed, for every meal
>   you eat alone

that tastes of me
so every painting

or story made by left hands
summon you and me

for new moons that turn
her back from your hands

I cast your nights dark

as the dead end you left
in a sweet witch's heart

Two Charlottes

i saw them in the flame
cascades of Divine
Feminine, long hair
around longing
oval faces, women
wrapped
      around
one another
      in our name

i saw them in the flame
two Charlottes
where blue wombs summon

the moths, in marigold
i saw our mothers meet

      mine pours yours Korbel
      yours unwraps endless red
      silk from her neck, a fire offering

      for the white buffalo behind the bar
      she spots her grit, former life
      stuffed beneath steel fingernails

so sanguine forges, blood
sacrament from her father
unhinging, same old

ancestor songs, unfolding

i saw them in the flame
mother words dressed
in me & you

i think i heard them say
they sent me to Decatur Street
to find you. To detangle
pirate girl knots, give healing
and my amethyst something to do

K.R. Morrison by Michelle Kilfeather. *Insta: @luckykilfeather*

K.R. Morrison is a poet and drummer who teaches English Literature and Creative Writing to inner city youth in San Francisco, Ca. In 1997, she fell in love with San Francisco, where she completed her B.A. in philosophy from USF (2001) a portion of which she earned at Oxford University, for Medieval Philosophy and Gothic Art and Architecture. Morrison earned a teaching credential, another B.A. in English Literature, and minored in Creative Writing from California State University, Long Beach (2004). Longing to return to the only place that ever felt like *home,* she went back to San Francisco, where she's been teaching at Galileo High School for 17 years.

Morrison was a guest on two popular Bay Area podcasts, *Bitchtalk* and *Storied: San Francisco* about being an educator, musician, and writer in a city that's rapidly changing. She has featured for many curations throughout the Bay Area, apart from reading at curations in New Orleans, Los Angeles, and New York. Published by Switchback, Quiet Lightning, and Haight Ashbury Literary Journal, Gasconade Review recently published three of her poems in an anthology entitled, *Ladies Night,* while Great Weather for Media included her "Memoir of a Pirate Girl Who Could and Did" in their most anthology, *Escape Wheel.*

Morrison writes and teaches online by the sea, a place she calls Mermaid Town. These days, her "home" is where the sea is, in the transition.

More
Paper Press
Books

Lumen de Lumine
Norman Dubie

Paris Blinks
Sharon Coleman

Poems About Something & Nothing
Karl Kempton

Church Retrospective
Missy Church

Murder
Michael Rothenberg

Armadillo Heart
M.K. Chavez & Cassandra Dallett

Notes From An Orgy
Paul Corman Roberts

Cineplex
Dennis Formento

Mrs. Jones Will Now Know
El Habib Louai

Lost Frames Compendium
Youssef Alaoui, Ed.

paperpressbooks.org/store

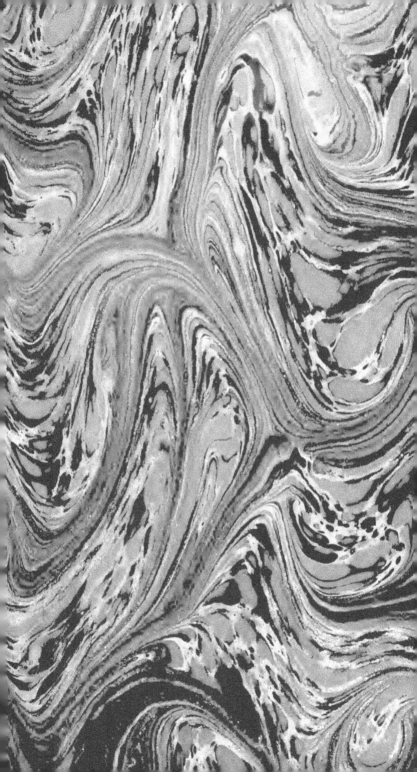

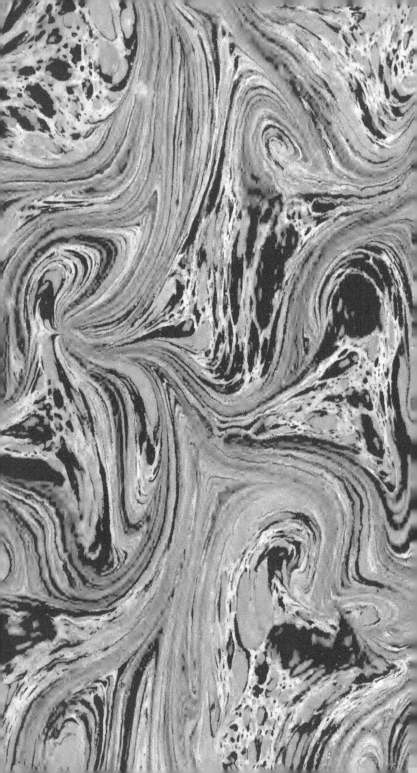

Printed in the USA
CPSIA information can be obtained
at www.ICGtesting.com
LVHW090359170524
780556LV00002B/149